The B-17G, Shoo Shoo Baby, *makes her last takeoff on October 15, 1988.*

THEN THE ENEMY COAST
SOON THE
ARE UP
(OUR NUMBER TWO MAN)
DATE 1943
FLIGHT FROM
FLIGHT TO
AND MODEL
AUG. 15 CHELVESTON FLUSHING, BELG. B-17F
AUG. 16 CHELVESTON PARIS, FRANCE
" 16 LOCAL
" 17 CHELVESTON SCHWIENFURT GREMANY
" 18 BASE TO MARTLESHAM HEATH AND RETURN
" 24 CHELVESTON TOPCLIFFE RETURN
" 27 BASE BOVINGTON RETURN
" 29
SEPT. 3 LOCAL
" 4 BASE WARTON RETURN
" 14 LOCAL
THE RECORD ON THIS PAGE IS CERTIFIED TRUE AND
PILOT
ATTESTED BY
BERLIN

THIS ONE CAME RIGHT THROUGH
FROM MIDNIGHT LEVEL
(OUR SQUADRON LEADER)
A SHIP HIT AND ON
FIRE - IT BLEW UP
SECONDS LATER
HIGH ATTACK
COMBAT TIME
WEIGHT-ENGINE CLASSIFICATION
DURATION OF FLIGHT
BREAKDOWN OF TRIP TIME INTO CLASSIFICATIONS
DAY
NIGHT
DUAL
SOLO
REMARKS
INSTRUCTOR SHOULD ENTER IN THIS COLUMN THE NATURE OF MANEUVER IN WHICH INSTRUCTION IS GIVEN, AND THE TIME THEREON, AND SHALL ATTEST EACH SUCH ENTRY WITH HIS PILOT CERTIFICATE NUMBER, AND PERTINENT RATING
636 VIRGIN
636 VIRGIN
23rd mission
24th mission
test Virgin 20,000'
25th. mission
cleaned out the VIRGIN
took Pete to school
trained new crews high altitude
CARRY TOTALS FORWARD TO TOP OF NEXT PAGE
CARRY TOTALS FORWARD TO TOP OF NEXT PAGE
ENTER IN THIS COLUMN DETAILS OF ANY SERIOUS DAMAGE TO AIRCRAFT. IF MORE SPACE THAN THAT PROVIDED ABOVE IS NEEDED FOR ANY DETAILS OF FLIGHT INSTRUCTION OR AIRCRAFT DAMAGE, USE PAGES PROVIDED IN BACK OF BOOK.

This book is dedicated to Mom and Dad, both veterans of what Dad refers to as, "The last big one."

First published 1993

ISBN 0 7110 2215 1

Printed and bound in Hong Kong.

Published by Ian Allan Ltd, Shepperton, Surrey.

Previous page: The personal logbook and scrapbook of Captain David Tyler of the 305th Bomb Group, based at Chevelston, England. Note that his 25th and last mission was to Schweinfurt, Germany, on August 17, 1943.

Shoo Shoo Baby *on the ramp at Wright Field, Dayton, Ohio.*

Preface

In the spring of 1966 during Mr. Bolger's seventh grade history class at Fairview Elementary School, I was called on to answer a question about the chapter we were discussing. Unfortunately I was reading a book hidden(or so I thought)in my desk that had nothing to do with what we were studying. Due to my lack of attention to the subject at hand, Mr. Bolger assigned the entire class an essay on paying attention and let everyone know that they had me to thank. I'd like to take this opportunity to apologize to my classmates and assure them that I was working on the book you are now holding. I read every book that I could find about the air wars over Europe during World War II, particularly about the men who flew and fought in the B-17.

I pored through those books, built models of the airplanes, and tried to imagine myself in those planes high in the sky over Europe. I never gave up on that dream and now have had the chance to illustrate the experiences of those crewmen through the photography and design of this book. The reality of the experiences those men had remains something that I can only imagine. I do know that after hours in these bombers taking photographs, I have unending respect for those crewmen and wonder how they got up in the morning, flew off to war in a machine with aluminum skin the thickness of a postcard, flown by kids through hostile skies, and maybe came back only to go again tomorrow.

Dan Patterson
November 18, 1992

L
483872
X
VP
X

THE LADY

Boeing B-17 Flying Fortress

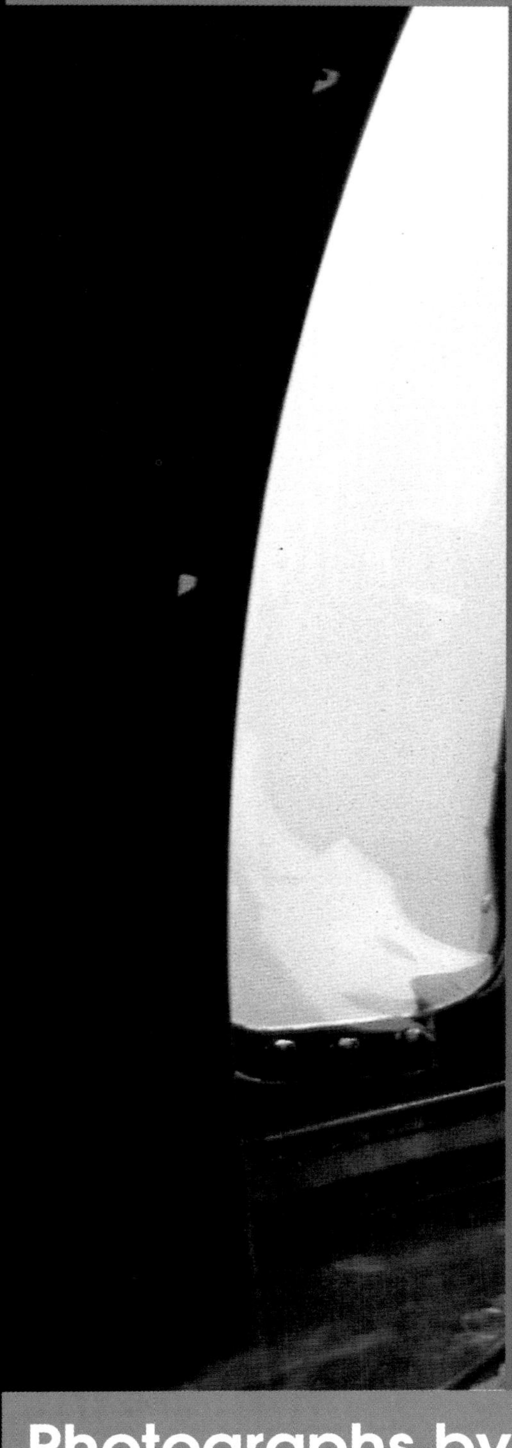

Photographs by Dan Patterson

Text by Paul Perkins

The Lady

"God, what a beautiful lady she is!"

It was September 1945, scant weeks after the end of WWII, when a B-17 took off from Patterson Field, near Dayton, Ohio. Whence it had come none of the onlookers really knew, and where it was headed they could only guess. Obviously "war weary," the Fort wore an olive drab paint job, albeit grimy, peeling, patched, and oil-stained. Still she was to the crowd "a beautiful lady."

This reaction was not unusual. Even to those who saw B-17s flying every day, there was something special about them. Perhaps it was the shape of the broad, graceful wings, or the sound of the four 1,200 horsepower Wright engines that made people look skyward. Maybe it was the Fort's reputation: well-mannered, honorable, and dignified. The B-17 war record was impressive; stories of her ability to withstand tremendous flak and fighter damage to get crews safely home were legion. Through all this she remained "a lady." To many she is still "the Queen."

In 1934, Wright Field issued Air Corps Circular Proposal 35-26, setting out requirements for a new multi-engine bomber to succeed the Martin B-10. The defensive role of this new bomber was defined by the isolationist attitudes of the time: quite simply, the United States would not get into any more foreign wars. However, on the off chance that somebody would be foolish enough to launch an attack across the vast expanse of our ocean borders, we would need defensive airplanes to patrol the coasts, intercept, and destroy hostile ships. Current wisdom held that no warplane would ever have the range to cross the oceans; but just a little over a decade before, Billy Mitchell had proved conclusively that ships could be sunk by aerial bombardment.

Circular Proposal 35-26 stipulated the new bomber must carry 2,000 pounds of bombs 1,020 miles at a top speed of 200 miles per hour. It did not specify the size of the bomber nor number of engines. At that time, "multi-engine" usually meant "two engines." Boeing made discrete inquiries whether or not four engines would be allowed.

Boeing Aircraft Corporation's rather daring response to the Air Corps circular was a calculated risk —a project that would culminate in the birth of the legendary B-17 "Flying Fortress." The B-17 did not arise from a single design vision as is sometimes implied. Rather, its origin was in three previous and ongoing Boeing projects: a very large, four-engine experimental bomber known as Project A, which would eventually become the XB-15; the Model 247 twin-engine transport the company had been supplying to the airlines since 1933; and the Model 300, a brand new four- engine transport that later would enter regular airline service as the Boeing 307 Stratoliner. With the Model 300 concept, Boeing had set aside for future reference some ideas for Model 299, a potential four-engine bomber using the same wing, engines, and tail structure. The risk in committing scarce funds to a melding of the XB-15, the Model 247, and the Model 300 was deemed worth the gamble — given the projected performance figures of the airplane.

On August 29, 1935, the Model 299 flew 2,100 miles nonstop from the Boeing plant in Seattle, Washington, to Wright Field near Dayton, Ohio, at an average speed of 233 miles per hour. Though the 299 was larger than the other two entries, the Douglas Aircraft Company's DB-1 and the Glenn L. Martin Company's Martin 146, the secret of this unbelievable performance lay, in contrast to former four-engine types, in the two extra engines providing power over and above that needed just to get airborne. The 299 carried a crew of eight, had five defensive gun positions, could deliver 4,800 pounds of bombs at 250 miles per hour, and boasted a range of 3,000 miles. It was obviously a lot more airplane than

Boeing Model 299. *USAFM*

had been requested. It was just as obviously, in the minds of some Air Corps leaders, exactly what was needed.

The Model 299 performed admirably in the Wright Field competition until October 30, 1935, when taken aloft with its innovative elevator locks still engaged. The locks worked — two crewmen died in the ensuing crash and fire. For a time it seemed that Project 299 would die as well.

The Douglas DB-1, given the designation B-18, won the competition almost by default. It is doubtful the outcome would have been different even had the Boeing 299 not crashed. The 299 was regarded as too big, complex, and expensive. The Boeing was much more airplane than was needed for requirements dictated by economic depression, isolationism, inter- and intra-service rivalries, funding battles, and traditional military thinking. In contrast, the performance and load-carrying capability of the B-18 were just what the Air Corps had requested. The aircraft was well suited for flying over water relatively close to shore — it was actually designed to float! Most important — the Douglas cost a lot less. At a time when quantity was all-important, the idea of getting two airplanes for just a little more than the price of one was very attractive.

The Model 299 and Boeing won a small victory when the Air Corps agreed to order thirteen service test models, plus a fourteenth airframe for structural testing. The service test contract was negotiated so soon after the crash of the prototype that these fourteen airplanes received a lower model designation number than the winner of the competition! (As an interesting footnote, the wreckage of the 299 was salvaged, including an intact section of the fuselage containing the side blisters used at Wright Field for developing the improved gun positions found on later B-17 models.)

Officially designated YB-17 and almost immediately redesignated Y1B-17 to reflect Federal funding separate from regular Air Corps appropriations, the new bomber had already garnered the popular name "Flying Fortress" because of its emphasis on defensive armament. A popular theory of the time, and one strongly influencing the B-17's design, held that unescorted mass formations of fast, heavily armed bombers could penetrate an enemy's airspace. Flying high would foil ground guns while speed would allow the aircraft to outrun any fighter the formation's incredible massed firepower could not discourage. The idea of any fighter escort was scorned. The term "flying fortresses" (no caps) described these mighty, theoretical bomber formations.

Seattle Times reporter Dick Williams supposedly applied the name "flying fortress" to the 299 on the occasion of its roll-out. Before the 299's first flight, Boeing registered "Flying Fortress" as the airplane's name. The Army Air Corps roster of aircraft nicknames, put together in October 1941 for use in public reference without revealing the aircraft's design status, shortened it to simply "Fortress." Nobody paid much attention. The theory of invincible bomber formations would be disproved during the B-17's operational career, but the name "Flying Fortress" would take on a whole new meaning in the public's imagination.

The thirteen Y1B-17s were practically identical to the original Model 299 except for their more powerful Wright R-1820 engines. For the time, the B-17s were considered heavily armed, with five .30- or (sometimes) .50-caliber machine guns, plus 8,000 pounds of bombs. Guns were mounted — one each — in the nose, the radio compartment for dorsal protection, a ventral blister, and two waist blisters. There was no tail defensive gun, and no notion that one would ever be needed.

The fourteenth Y1B-17 was procured solely as a non-flying structural test model. However, after another Y1B-17

Boeing Model 299 over Wright Field. *USAFM*

inadvertently flew into a severe thunderstorm and escaped intact, the planned static tests were deemed unnecessary and canceled. This aircraft, designated Y1B-17A, became the flying test-bed for the exhaust-driven turbosupercharger that replaced the two-stage gear-driven supercharger, then standard on the Wright Cyclone engines. After completion of the service test phase, the Y1B-17A became the B-17A, and all Y1B-17s were redesignated B-17.

Twelve of the thirteen former Y1B-17s were assigned operationally to the Second Bombardment Group at Langley Field, Virginia, under the command of Colonel Robert Olds. Before acceptance by the Air Corps as a defensive weapon, the

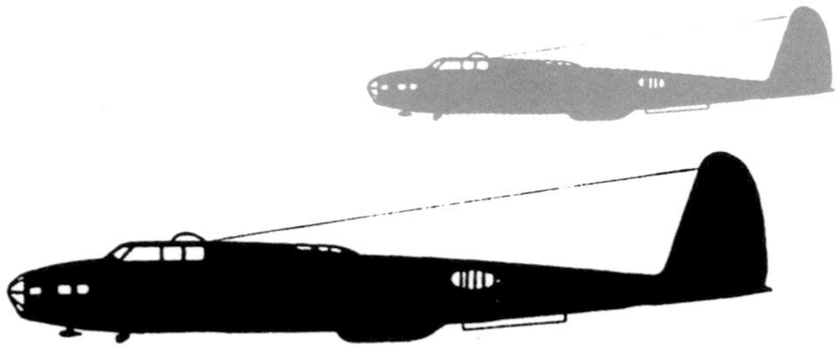

B-17 and its crews and ground support personnel would have to define their mission and demonstrate their capabilities. The burden of this task fell upon Colonel Olds. He orchestrated a multitude of exercises, goodwill and record-setting flights, that not only garnered favorable publicity for the Fortress, but also provided vital operational training in instrument flying (a fairly new concept) and over-water navigation for pilots and crews. He organized and ran his command as if it were going to war at any minute. Serving under Colonel Olds in the 2nd Bomb Group was then-Lieutenant Curtis LeMay, who would apply many of the lessons learned at that time when he became commander-in-chief of Strategic Air Command in October 1948.

Naturally, the Navy felt threatened by Colonel Olds' success with the new warplanes as he intercepted and "bombed" vessels on open ocean. A gentlemen's agreement was struck which limited bomber operations to within 100 miles of shore. There was a bright side to this: keeping within the 100-mile limit required very precise navigation!

Early series B-17s were built in relatively small quantities, reflecting the tenor of the times, the B-17B being the first real production model of the Fortress. Except for revised control surfaces and nose arrangement, the thirty-nine B-17Bs were outwardly similar to the Y1B-17s. Armament remained essentially the same, although some B-17Bs were field modified to add different gun mountings in the nose. Turbosuperchargers were added to the engines of these and all subsequent B-17 models.

The B-17Cs were similar to B-17Bs with the exception of defensive armament arrangements, and a decrease in bomb load to 4,000 pounds. The single gun socket in the nose bubble was replaced by a socket in either side window. Flush gunports were substituted for the waist blisters, and the ventral blister was exchanged for a metal "bathtub" type housing that could accommodate either one or two guns. Twin .50 - caliber guns were generally installed in the upper and lower positions. Twenty of the thirty-eight B-17Cs built were transferred to Britain as Fortress Is. Intended for use in training, these aircraft were flown on very high-altitude bombing sorties in insufficient numbers for mutual protection. The results were disastrous. The RAF concluded that the Fortress could neither outrun, outgun, nor outmaneuver the German fighters. Not only was the defensive armament insufficient, but the aircraft demonstrated poor directional stability at high altitudes — corrected with the redesigned tail of the B-17E. While this distinctive

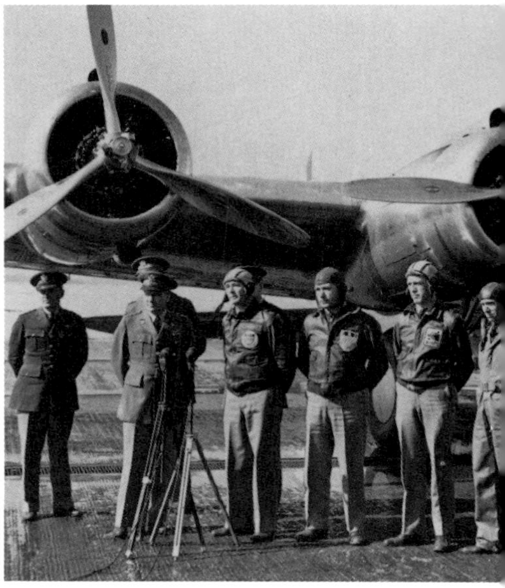

Colonel Olds and his crew. USAFM

broad tail of later B-17s resulted in a superbly stable bomb-aiming and delivery platform, it also complicated taxiing with a crosswind.

The B-17D was similar to its predecessors with few external modifications. Internal changes included electrical improvements and the addition of a crew member. Although the B-17Cs and B-17Ds were delivered in the standard bare-metal finish and markings of the Army Air Corps, the aircraft were given camouflage paint at Air Corps depots. Most of the B-17Ds in the Pacific were destroyed on the ground by the Japanese raids on Pearl Harbor and the Philippines. Twelve B-17Ds from California carrying extra fuel, spare parts, and support equipment in place of guns, arrived over Oahu right in the midst of the attack on Pearl Harbor. They were badly shot up. It was the B-17D that participated in the first American bombing raid of the war, when three of them sortied against Japanese shipping on December 10, 1941. The early experiences of B-17s in the Pacific, many of which had little to do with bombing, prompted the Japanese to refer to them as a "fighting plane used for all purposes."

The B-17E was the first model produced in quantity. The 512 examples featured a vastly redesigned tail with dorsal

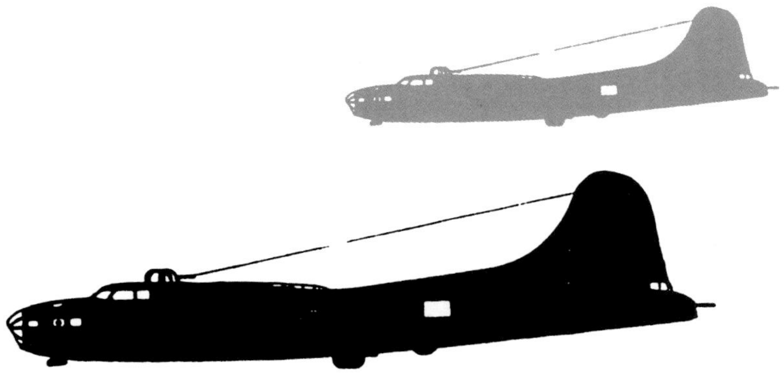

fin to accommodate a tail gunner and his two weapons. The standard fighter attack from behind with an overtaking speed of 100 miles per hour took just eighteen seconds to close the distance from 1,000 to 100 yards. It was an abbreviated eighteen seconds for some surprised Japanese fighter pilots. Other armament improvements included a new powered upper turret with twin .50-caliber guns and a remotely aimed Sperry ventral turret. This was replaced in later -E blocks by a manned ball turret with twin .50s.

On July 4, 1942, the first Army Air Force B-17Es arrived in England. Pilots had received very little instruction in the art of formation flying, and the gunners even less schooling in their trade. The first order of business was four weeks of intensive training. On August 17, 1942, the B-17E became the first of the Fortresses to see action with American forces in Europe with a daylight raid made by twelve bombers on Rouen, France. Six other B-17Es participated in a diversionary mission against St. Omer. Operations against Germany proper began on January 27, 1943, with the Wilhelmshaven raid — when most of the B-17Es had been replaced by newer B-17F models.

With the introduction of the B-17F in May 1942, Vega and Douglas joined Boeing in Fortress production. The "BVD" manufacturing pool produced a total of 3,400 B-17Fs. Since the Army system of designation did not specify who built which aircraft, a suffix added to the block designation indicated the manufacturer (BO for Boeing, DL - Douglas/Long Beach, VE - Vega). Additional numbers indicated minor ongoing modifications carried out on production lines or at modification centers all over the country. The B-17F was the first series of B-17 to carry these additional block designations.

The B-17F featured a molded Plexiglas nose with two cheek guns and sometimes a third nose gun firing directly forward. An additional .50-caliber gun could be fired through the removable skylight of the radio compartment. Later B-17Fs had extra nine-celled fuel tanks in the outer wings. These so-called "Tokyo Tanks" carried another 1,100 gallons of fuel.

Before long-range escort fighters, "Little Friends," were available, 20 B-17Fs (designation YB-40) were built. These had extra armor around the tail and twin .50-caliber waist positions, a power turret with twin .50-caliber at the radio room position, and a Bendix remotely operated "chin turret" carrying two .50-caliber machine guns. With all that extra weight in armor, guns, and twice the normal ammunition, YB-40s were hard pressed to maintain formation inbound to the target. A YB-40 departing a target was as heavy as when it arrived. German fighters picked on stragglers — and the firepower of YB-40s was of no help to them. Moreover, a YB-40 that lost an engine ran a real risk of becoming a straggler itself. The project was abandoned.

The B-17F's vulnerability to head-on attacks was answered in 1943 when the "BVD" pool commenced producing the B-17G series. Its innovative defensive armament was headlined by the Bendix remotely operated chin turret earlier fitted to the YB-40s. Most pilots considered the corresponding performance loss caused by the extra weight and drag of a chin turret fair trade for the increased forward firepower. In addition, there was one .50-caliber gun in each side of the nose in a staggered "cheek" position. The waist gun positions were also staggered in later B-17G models to reduce interference between the gunners, and many were fitted with closed waist windows and gun mounts. The last definitive B-17 series of original manufacture was also the most prolific; 8,680 B-17Gs saw almost exclusive service in the ETO.

The B-17, with its relatively easy handling and high-altitude capability, was well suited for the environment over "Fortress Europe." Large, tight formations flying at high altitudes to avoid heavy ground fire were the norm. The formation was the key to survival. It was intended to

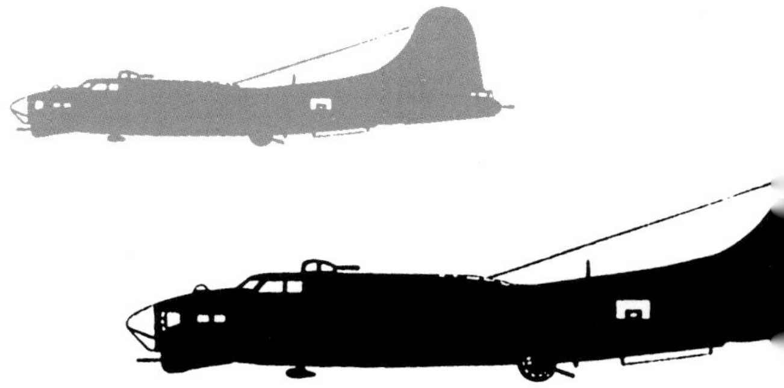

yield maximum interlocking defensive firepower, bomb saturation, and prevent the high squadron from bombing the low squadron.

The most frequently used formation was the combat box, pioneered for the AAF by then-Colonel Curtis LeMay, later modified as experience warranted and made standard for the Eighth Air Force. The basic unit consisted of two or more Vs of

Elements of the Eighth Air Force in combat boxes over Europe. *390th Collection*

three bombers each, one trailing the other, all at slightly different altitudes. Sometimes a seventh "tail-end Charlie" aircraft was added to the rear, to "fill in the diamond." The usual configuration used by the Eighth Air Force was a "V of Vs" of 18 - 21 aircraft comprising three of these units, with one trailing formation stacked high and the other, low. The resulting formation was referred to variously as the "Combat Box," the "Group Combat Box," or the "Group." This arrangement made optimum use of each component aircraft's guns while allowing flexibility to adapt to changing combat conditions, such as tightening the formation after the loss of one or more of its aircraft. (Prop wash made flat formations impossible, and staggered altitudes increased the difficulty for ground gunners to hit their targets.) Generally, three combat boxes comprised the combat wing, and any number of these could be combined into a striking force.

Maintaining tight formation for ten or more hours was difficult, particularly when being harassed by fighters and flak. A good formation demanded constant concentration and cooperation of all the pilots. The aircraft commander of the lead crew set the speed for the entire formation. Set the speed too fast and groups taking off from other stations would have difficulty catching up. Set the speed too slow and the time under threat from flak would be unnecessarily prolonged. Wheeling a formation through the sky in a majestic turn was not as simple as a trained squadron made it appear. The leader could fly constant throttle, thus conserving fuel — meanwhile the aircraft inside the radius of the formation's turn had to slow down while those on the outside had to speed up. In some cases, an experienced pilot substituted for the tail gunner in the lead aircraft to monitor the status of the rest of the formation.

The lead crew concept was another of LeMay's innovations to improve navigation and bombing accuracy. The best of a group's navigators and bombardiers were assigned specific target areas for intensive study. After hours poring over aerial photos and sand table models, flying dozens of practice missions in ground trainers, each team could recognize its target from any altitude and direction. Thus, the lead crew for a mission was chosen based upon a crew's area of specialization, frequently with the mission commander as pilot, the regular pilot as copilot, and the copilot riding the tail gun position as observer.

Unescorted raids on targets such as Schweinfurt and Regensburg revealed that box formations with interlocking fields of defensive fire were not enough to prevent crippling losses of men and machines. Improved fighter technology and tactics were factors — but there were errors in the theory that were even more basic. No one had thought to allow for the varying skill and experience of the pilots, physical and mental fatigue from hours of maintaining tight formation, or the defensive integrity of the formation being degraded by the loss of any of its components. Enemy fighters quickly adopted head-on attacks and learned to single out individual squadrons, hammering that particular box in an attempt to degrade the defensive fire. A crippled bomber that could not keep formation was, by necessity, left to the not-so-tender mercies of the Luftwaffe.

Originally envisioned for coastal defense and the interception and destruction of invading enemy ships, the B-17 performed that role during the Battle of Midway, June 4, 1942. While the bombing performance of the seventeen aircraft was less than sterling, they proved their worth for long-distance tactical reconnaissance. The Navy was sufficiently impressed that it canceled many patrol flying boats and ordered four-engine land planes — long-range B-24s, not B-17s!

The Luftwaffe flew a handful of captured B-17s for a variety of purposes. Mostly, they were studied and flown to help perfect offensive tactics. There were, however, reports of "stragglers" joining bomber formations to radio position and altitude reports to waiting fighters and ground defenses. When was a Dornier not a Dornier? Luftwaffe squadron KG 200 flew at least six different B-17s (referring to them as Do 200s) in clandestine operations, such as delivering agents and equipment to the Middle East and North Africa. The Germans cannibalized downed aircraft for spares to keep their captured planes flying. Metal from wrecked airframes also found its way into new fighters for the Luftwaffe.

A major instrument of the strategic air offensive in the ETO — the B-17 was overrun by events and aeronautical advances. The successor to the B-17, the B-29 Superfortress, was the only bomber assigned to Strategic Air Command (SAC) when it was established in 1946.

Most remaining B-17s were torched in the postwar demobilization frenzy. Some were "retired," waiting in storage to be salvaged or recalled to active duty. Those that continued in service officially were aircraft modified for specific tasks. B-17s flew in Army Air Corps, Air Force, Navy, and Coast Guard service until 1960 as transports (CB-17 or VB-17), in high-altitude mapping (RB-17), weather reconnaissance (WB-17G), radar early warning (PB-1W), and drones (QB-17). Ironically, the last of these drones was destroyed by a Boeing Bomarc surface-to-air missile in 1960.

A wartime B-17G conversion worthy of note was the B-17H. Twelve examples, later redesignated SB-17G, were for air-sea rescue work and featured a lifeboat slung underneath which could be dropped by parachute to a downed crew. Those deployed to combat zones retained their defensive armament, while others had armament removed and radar installed in place of the chin turret. These were the last Fortresses in regular squadron service with the USAF; the 57th Air Rescue Squadron was based in the Azores until 1956. SB-17Gs serving in the Korean conflict were also the last armed Fortresses in U.S. service.

Surplus B-17s also were sold either on the civilian market or to foreign governments. Though most were used as transports, aerial spray planes, or fire fighters, three B-17s purchased by Israel were employed as bombers against Egypt in 1949, then again in 1956. The French *l'Institut Geographic National* operated a small number of B-17s for more than thirty years in high-altitude photographic mapping.

A three - plane element of B-17s. 390th Collection

The first conversion of a B-17 as an "air tanker" for fire fighting was completed in June 1960. Two aluminum tanks, having a total capacity of 1,800 gallons, were mounted to the bomb bay and the bomb rails, using existing bolt holes. Each tank was divided in the middle to create four 450-gallon compartments, and each compartment further divided by perforated baffles to reduce any surge that might be produced during flight. Each compartment had its own door in the bottom; the chemical fire-fighting "slurry" (borate and water, mostly, hence the nickname "Borate Bomber") could be dropped from these separately or in a salvo. Twenty-three "Borate Bombers" were built for the United States Forest Service. Their job was to sit "on alert" at designated airfields during the fire season. In the event of a forest fire, they would fly into their assigned area at roughly 150 feet above the blazing trees, laying a fire-retardant slurry (which usually also contained an orange-red dye for visibility and a fertilizer to speed regrowth) on the ground alongside the flames. It was hazardous duty. Low-speed, low-altitude, precision "bombing" over rough terrain through turbulence and smoke claimed at least one aircraft per season. These aircraft served until the early 1980s!

According to Army Air Force records, there were 12,726 B-17s built, counting the Model 299 and all aircraft carrying the designation B-17 in original manufacture. All told, the series had an operational U.S. military life of more than a quarter century. Of the roughly 12,700 B-17s manufactured, only a small number are preserved in museums around the world, and an even smaller number are still flying.

The Air Crew

The combat air crew was a special group of men, welded by pride, skill, teamwork, and fighting spirit. Often the crew assembled stateside, trained together, shipped out together either by sea or in a brand-new airplane, and served together once overseas. They did not always stay together — the likelihood of completing a 25-mission combat tour in 1943 was about 35%. Crew changes occurred due to casualties, illnesses, mission requirements, and personality clashes — but once a crew was formed, its members tried to remain a team.

Pilot

The pilot of the B-17 was the airplane commander. The B-17 and crew were his charges. The airplane commander was responsible for the safety and efficiency of the crew at all times — not just when flying and fighting, but for the full twenty-four hours of every day he was in command.

The crew was made up of specialists. How well each member did his job, what he contributed as a member of the combat team, greatly depended on how well the pilot played his part as the airplane commander. The pilot needed to know each member of the crew as an individual, his personal idiosyncrasies, capabilities, and shortcomings. He had to take a personal interest in their problems, their ambitions, and their individual needs for special training. Like the commander of any force, large or small, he set the tone for morale.

Success as airplane commander depended in large measure on the respect, confidence, and trust the crew felt for him. Part of the glue that held a crew together was discipline. The pilot's position commanded obedience and respect. It did not afford him the luxury of being stubborn, overbearing, or aloof.

The pilot needed to be friendly, understanding, but firm. He needed to understand his job and duty — and to convince the crew that he knew his stuff. He had to be fair and impartial in his decisions. The decision — once made — had to be final. Respect for the aircraft commander needed to arise out of respect for him as an individual — not the position he held. Crew discipline bred comradeship and high morale as natural byproducts.

The crew needed to be briefed for every flight: the purpose of the flight, conditions that might be encountered, and the role each member needed to play for mission success. Crew training ensured that every member was thoroughly familiar with his duties in the event of emergency.

The airplane commander was coach in a sport with mortal stakes.

Engine #1 smoking.

David A. Tyler

Copilot

The copilot was the pilot's executive officer, chief understudy, and strong right hand (both figuratively and literally). He had to be familiar with all the pilot's responsibilities and duties. The American practice of assigning two men to fly the plane, deemed extravagant by some, was vindicated in combat. Promotion, courtesy of fighters or AAA, meant the copilot would have to fly the B-17 with the same skill as the pilot. Though not in direct command of engine controls, he had to understand their operation to ensure smooth operation in cruise, maintaining or changing formation position, climb, and descent. He was an engineering officer aboard the airplane, maintaining a complete log of performance data.

He was a qualified instrument pilot — able to fly good formation in any assigned position, day or night. He had to be proficient at navigation, day or night, by pilotage, dead reckoning, or by radio aids (primarily the radio in the cockpit).

Copilots frequently went on to take over their own ships and crews with mixed emotions, proud to assume command — regretful at leaving the old team. A good pilot facilitated this transition by giving his copilot his fair share of flying responsibility.

Radio Operator

The radio operator had the least glamorous job in a B-17. He had a compartment in the center of the fuselage with the doors open fore and aft to communicate with the rest of the crew. This fellow sat for hours on end, static crackling in his ears, giving position reports every thirty minutes, assisting the navigator in taking fixes, and informing headquarters of targets attacked and results. Sending any distress signals was his responsibility. He maintained the equipment in good working order, maintained a log, preflighted the radio equipment, and frequently acted as the crew photographer. There was a hatch in the radio compartment roof for a single .50-caliber machine gun. (This position had a very limited field of fire and was discontinued.) Finally, the radio operator was responsible for the first-aid equipment he fervently hoped would stay unused.

Engineer

The engineer had to know more about the B-17 than any member of the crew — including the airplane commander. He was senior enlisted man aboard. To be a qualified combat engineer a man had to know his airplane, his engines, and his armament thoroughly. The lives of the entire crew, the safety of the equipment, and the success of a mission rested squarely on his shoulders. In emergencies, it was the engineer to whom the airplane commander turned.

Ideally, the airplane commander taught the engineer as much as possible about flying — reasoning that the more complete the engineer's understanding of the function of the equipment — the more valuable the engineer would be if and when something went wrong. He was well versed on all emergency procedures, and could assist in flying the aircraft when necessary.

He had to work closely with the copilot, checking engine operation, fuel consumption, and the operation of all equipment. He had to work with the bombardier to cock, lock, and load the bomb racks.

He had to be thoroughly familiar with the armament equipment, and know how to strip, clean, and reassemble the guns.

His was the most comfortable defensive position to fly in the B-17. From the top turret he could usually see any enemy plane positioning to attack and alert the other gunners.

Bombardier

Accurate and effective bombing was the ultimate purpose of the B-17 and crew. Every other function was preparatory to hitting and destroying a target. Getting the bombardier over the target was a vital part of the exercise. The bombardier's job, putting bombs on the target, required close cooperation with the pilot and a mutual understanding of duties. During the brief interval (usually less than three minutes) of the bomb run — the bombardier was in absolute command. He told the airplane commander what was needed: until the bombs left the racks his word was law. The bombardier controlled the aircraft on the bomb run, either through the auto-pilot or Pilot Directional Indicator (PDI). The auto-pilot connected directly to the bombsight; the PDI transmitted desired course changes to the pilot via a needle instrument on the cockpit panel.

The bombing problem was a function of many variables.

1. *Altitude,* controlled by the pilot, determined the length of time the bombs were in flight and affected by atmospheric conditions. The forward travel of the bombs (range) and deflection (distance the bombs drifted in a crosswind with respect to the aircraft's ground track) were a function of time from release to impact. The altimeter needed to be calibrated and correct — and the pilot had to maintain the assigned altitude as accurately as possible. For every additional 100 feet above the assumed bombing altitude of 20,000 feet, bombing error increased by thirty feet.

A 390th Bomb Group B-17G over Europe. *390th Collection*

2. *True airspeed,* controlled by the pilot, was the measure the B-17's speed through the air. The true airspeed of the bomb determined the trail of the bomb — the horizontal distance the bomb lagged behind the bomber at the moment of impact. Once the bombing airspeed and altitude were entered into the bombsight — they had to be maintained. For erroneous airspeed, bombing error in-

creased approximately 170 feet for a ten MPH change.

3. *Bomb ballistics* tables for each type of bomb described their intended trajectory from bomber to target.

4. *Trail,* mentioned earlier, was available from bombing tables and set in the bombsight by the bombardier. Trail was affected by altitude, airspeed, bomb ballistics, and air density — the first two factors being controlled by the pilot.

5. *Actual time* of fall was affected by altitude, type of bomb, and air density.

6. *Ground speed,* the speed of the B-17 in relation to the earth's surface, affected the range of the bomb and varied with airspeed, controlled by the pilot.

7. *Drift,* determined by the direction and velocity of the wind, was the distance the bomb traveled downwind from the aircraft on its journey to the target. Drift was set on the bombsight by the bombardier.

During a bomb run, flak and fighter opposition were to be "ignored." Multiple head-on attacks by Bf 109s and Fw 190s, their nose and wing leading edges twinkling with cannon and machine-gun fire — were to be ignored. The wall of angry flak blossoms was to be ignored. German fighter pilots did not always leave the bombers to deal with AA over the target. There were valorous instances where they pressed home their attacks through their own flak.

The best area bombing results were achieved by having a lead bombardier sight for the whole formation. The rest of the formation's bombardiers "toggled," released their bombs, precisely on the lead bombardier's drop or marker.

Navigator

The navigator was tasked with getting the plane to and from the objective, furnishing the pilot with flight directions, keeping the flight log book, and manning a nose gun in the event of fighter attack. He needed to be well versed on weather, flak concentrations, and what formation was being used.

Navigation was a combination of dead reckoning (using speed and elapsed time between checkpoints to compute position), pilotage (watching the ground for visible landmarks), radio use, and celestial navigation. The B-17 navigator had his own Plexiglas bubble just forward of the cockpit through which he could shoot his fixes. Celestial navigation was usually used only when delivering the aircraft to theater. In combat navigation, all bombing targets were approached by pilotage. The position accuracy expected was one- quarter mile.

Instrument calibration was an important duty of the navigator — since all navigation and bombing depended directly on the accuracy of his instruments. Correct calibration required close cooperation and extremely careful flying by the pilot. Instruments to be calibrated included the altimeter, compasses, airspeed indicator, astrocompass, astrograph, drift meter, and sextant.

Before the mission the pilot and navigator studied the route to be flown and selected alternate airfields. The pilot advised the navigator on weather expected and the airspeed and altitude that the mission was to be flown. Checkpoints were discussed. Once in the air, the pilot needed to fly consistent airspeed and course — and notify the navigator of any changes. Though the formation depended on the lead navigator, it was essential that all navigators monitor compass headings and have some idea of their position in case something happened to the lead ship (a priority target for flak or fighters), or they themselves had to leave the formation. The navigator was expected to give the pilot position reports at regular intervals.

Additional duties of the navigator included familiarity with the oxygen system, turrets, fuel transfer system, and radios. He had to know the location of all fuses and spare fuses, lights, and spare lights, affecting navigation. He was well versed with emergency procedures such

B-17Fs of the 390th Bomb Group. *390th Collection*

as crash landings, bailing out, ditching, and manual operation of the landing gear, bomb doors, and flaps.

Gunners

The number of gunners, along with those already mentioned, usually remained at four for the B-17. All gunners necessarily were well-trained in aircraft identification, possessed a good sense of timing, and needed to know where to place their hits for maximum effect. With high rates of closure, evasive action, and the rolling and pitching of the bomber through turbulent air, it was difficult, if not impossible, to get a decent shot — though the combined effect of hundreds of guns was deadly. The policy of awarding "kills" to gunners differed among commands; some recognized claims that could be substantiated by eyewitnesses, some did not. The official decision of the USAF History Office was not to recognize claims from gunners in WW II bombers, due to the obvious problems surrounding confirmation.

Waist gunners had the distinction of manning the position with the most casualties. It was the least well protected, and frostbite was a major concern. They had to wrestle 65-pound Browning machine guns against a slipstream of 150+ MPH while taking care not to entangle themselves in oxygen, inter phone, and electric connections, or slip on brass shell casings piling up around their feet.

Small men were generally chosen as ball turret gunners. There was no room for a parachute in this cramped position. The gunner kept his Sperry-built power turret in constant rotation on look-out and to aim. The gunner usually did not climb in until well after takeoff, and climbed out again before landing. Though definitely not for the acro- or claustrophobic, the ball turret was statistically the safest position, from the standpoint of numbers and types of battle wounds. The lonely man in the ball turret of a B-17 was, however, least likely to escape should catastrophe occur.

B-17Gs of the 390th Bomb Group. *390th Collection*

The tail gunner in the B-17 crawled around the tail wheel well to then kneel on a bicycle seat to fire his weapon. His job was to watch for fighters closing from behind as well as to monitor the formation. During takeoff or landing, the ball turret and tail gunners generally occupied positions in the radio compartment. The ball turret gunner was out from underneath the aircraft for obvious reasons of safety. The tail gunner, with his allotment of ammunition, was there to reduce the inherent tail-heaviness of the B-17.

For the air crew, working conditions meant routinely spending two to twelve hours in a shaking metal box, in sub-zero temperatures, with oxygen masks rubbing the skin off faces, and incessant engine noise making conversation impossible except by inter phone. The intense cold blasting in through open gun apertures was somewhat countered by heaters and bulky electric flying suits. According to some reports, frostbite outnumbered all other combat injuries. Consider the stress of sitting inside a target locked in a formation position. Most crew members agreed that the flak was far worse to endure than fighter attacks (though they would have preferred to encounter neither). They couldn't fight those 30-yard-across black puffs blossoming all around them, nor side-step the shrapnel that routinely ripped through the aluminum skin of the fuselage. There were almost no evasive maneuvers possible as fighters bore down upon them — but at least they had their defensive firepower.

What if your aircraft were mortally wounded? The best you could do was dismiss that possibility. It wouldn't happen to you or your plane. The Fort and your skipper would always get you home. When the unthinkable occurred, the pilot would attempt to hold the plane straight and level so that everyone could get clear. Getting clear meant not hitting the tail of the airplane, being struck by debris, or smashing into an aircraft as you plummeted through the formation. Spins were the most feared, for once established the centrifugal force pinned the crew inside — while the altimeter wound down. Even if

Mission preparation, B-17F, 305th Bomb Group. David A. Tyler

a parachute blossomed over your head and you had escaped the chaos above, there were new dangers. Depending on your initial altitude and descending at 1,000 feet per minute, you had a long ride to the ground — a long time to think about what you would find when you arrived. You would either be in the water, praying that air-sea rescue would find you before the enemy or sharks, or on the ground in enemy territory, facing hostile civilians and possible internment by the German or Japanese military.

Ground Crew

An AAF heavy bomber consisted of as many as 12,000 individual parts, any of which could require replacement due to battle damage or wear. Service and repair personnel of a squadron were organized into ground crews, each normally responsible for service and maintenance of a particular B-17. The complexity of a "modern instrument of war," the B-17, was reflected by the number of enlisted ground crew specialists: supercharger, power plant, fabric and dope, electrical instrument, automatic pilot instrument, fire control instrument, gyro instrument, optical instrument, hydraulic, machinists, parachute riggers, propeller, sheet metal working, welders, and woodworkers. This is probably an incomplete list. Each crew was supervised by a crew chief — the crew chiefs were supervised by a line chief — a master sergeant.

Army Air Corps maintenance was divided into four echelons. First echelon maintenance consisted of servicing (fueling) airplanes and equipment; preflight and daily inspections;and minor repairs (tightening nuts, bolts, and hose clamps), adjustments, and replacements. Second echelon maintenance was performed by the ground crew of the combat unit and airdrome squadrons. Responsibilities consisted of servicing airplanes and equipment, periodic preventive inspections, and such adjustments, repairs, and replacements as could be accomplished by hand tools and mobile equipment. Second echelon maintenance would include checking timing, adjusting valves, and changing engines. Third echelon maintenance was performed by the base maintenance organization in the U.S. and the service centers in overseas theaters. Responsibilities included field repairs and salvage, removal and replacement of major unit assemblies, fabrication of minor parts, and minor repairs to aircraft structures. Normally these repairs were made getting the plane ready for the next mission. Fourth echelon maintenance was done at an air depot apart from the regular B-17 base. Responsibilities included complete restoration of worn or damaged aircraft, periodic overhaul of assemblies and accessories, fabrication of parts required to supplement normal supply, technical modifications, and final disposition of reclaimed and salvaged materials.

Preventive inspection was to prevent accident, damage, or part failure before it occurred. The maintenance inspection record was a complete logbook of each airplane's operations and maintenance. It contained the record of flying time and specified times for oil and engine changes. Inspections were made before every flight; daily; after 25, 50, and 100 hours of flight; at time of engine change; 25 hours after engine change; and at special periods as required by specific models of aircraft. These inspections were progressively more involved and thorough — by the 500-hour inspection, every part and accessory had been checked. A 25-hour inspection of a B-17 required about 100 man-hours, and a 100-hour inspection could take 400 man-hours.

Nothing was thrown away. In fact, in most theaters, a major source of spares was planes damaged in action. When a plane could no longer be kept flyable, the usable parts were stripped and either immediately used or stocked. The AAF called this "reclamation;" the field expression was "cannibalization."

Few aircraft returned from a major

Bomb dump, 390th Bomb Group. *390th Collection*

combat mission without some damage from flak or enemy aircraft. One shell through the fuselage of a heavy bomber could damage multiple systems.

Consider one hypothetical daylight bombing attack against a well-defended target by a force of 150 bombers and 75 escort fighters. Assume 10 aircraft lost over enemy territory; 6 forced to land at alternate airfields; 25 extensively damaged; 50 moderately damaged; 25 with minor damages; and 109 unscathed. The 6 forced landings would require about 7,200 man- hours for maintenance; the 25 extensively damaged would average 450 man-hours apiece, totaling 11,250 man-hours; the 50 moderately damaged at an average of 300 man-hours, would require 15,000 man-hours; and the 25 slightly damaged, averaging 150 man-hours, would total 3,750 man-hours. The total maintenance required for repairs alone (not service) would be 37,200 man-hours, or a 48-hour work week for 775 men. Remember that missions frequently involved more than 150 bombers and one can begin to appreciate the enormous effort involved keeping the B-17 fleet combat ready.

Though air crew were the "glory guys," ground crews considered the aircraft they worked on as their own, only borrowed by air crews for a mission. Ground crews took great pride in their aircraft's appearance and performance. Much of the maintenance and repair work was done at night, outside, in all kinds of weather, preparing for the next morning's mission. On mission day the ground crews were responsible for a host of details, from cleaning the noses and all other Plexiglas, to warming up the engines and doing preflight walk-around inspections with the pilots.

For their own part, in all theaters of operation, maintenance troops battled mud, dust, sand, excessive heat, bitter cold, and humidity that ate away at both metal and men. They endured stuffy tents, freezing wooden barracks, insects, snakes, and the possibility of enemy attack. They made do without — or improvised. Exhaustion brought on by 24-hour work days was common. While the flyboys rotated home after a set number of combat hours or missions, the ground crews were there for the duration. There was little hope of promotions, medals, or recognition other than the thanks of their grateful air crews.

Yet, if asked, they would say their most difficult task was watching plane after plane take off and waiting out the mission — with frequent glances at the sky, ears straining to hear the welcome drone of approaching engines, wondering how many aircraft they would count on the group's return.

Whether flying the missions or sweating them out on the ground, Army Air Corps personnel came to regard aircraft as entities with names and personalities all their own. But how can one explain to the uninitiated the affection of an air or ground crew member for a particular airplane? How does one describe the sense of loyalty to a machine that would make a crew chief refuse the weekend pass that would mean leaving "his" airplane in someone else's hands? How could collections of metal, rubber, and petrochemicals be viewed as possessing personalities? How could certain aircraft be considered lucky and others jinxed?

These were not living creations — they were instruments of war. But they were instruments created and animated by people. As a team — the common link between air crew and ground crew was the airplane. The ground crew did everything possible to get the airplane and air crew to the target and back. Once handed over to the air crew, the airplane was more than a conveyance — it was the instrument of their purpose and survival. The B-17 carried a generation of people into carnage they could never have imagined possible. The air crew took the B-17 into harm's way and back. The ground crew healed the wounds. What happens when the lives and fortunes of that many people focused upon a machine? The machine began taking on a life of its own.

RACK SELECTOR

A

Previous page: Behind the bombardier's seat, to the left, is the control panel that gave him the necessary information to program the bombsight. Altimeter reads 5,500 feet. The switches control the bomb bay doors and arm the bombs. Lights give the status of the bomb load. The intervalometer is at bottom left. This controlled the timing of bomb release — either a salvo (all bombs at once) or at intervals to "walk" the bombs across the target. In the center is the Norden bombsight. This bombsight, a closely guarded secret during WWII, computed aircraft flight variables and bomb ballistics to arrive at a solution — a point in space from which the bombs could be released to strike the target. To the right is a "cheek" .50-caliber heavy machine gun manned by the bombardier before and after the bomb run.

A. Nine other men flew and fought to put the bomber and this man in position to destroy the target.

B. The bombardier crouches over his bombsight. To the right in the stowed position is the control for the chin turret. Another B-17 flies formation ahead.

C. The Norden bombsight.

USAFM

(In above and subsequent diagrams, gray area denotes aircraft section depicted in photographs.)

B

C

A

A. The navigator's tools spread across his table in the nose compartment. His job was to keep the pilot informed of position, and any upcoming course changes, and to know the course back to base from any point of the mission. Through a combination of pilotage and dead reckoning (visual landmarks and time—distance), with these tools he kept track of their progress. Besides these duties he manned a machine gun visible at the top of the photo.

B. To enter the nose compartment,the crewman had to crawl through a passage under the cockpit floor,past an escape hatch and through a small opening in the bulkhead. This is the view forward as he crawled into the nose. Left is the navigator's table and chair. The cheek guns are in ball mounts, suspended by a system of springs and cables to make them easier to move while tracking enemy fighters.

C. Engines #3 and #4 viewed through the navigator's side window.

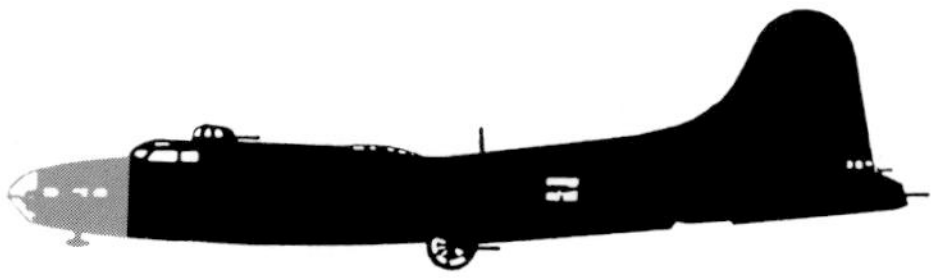

USAFM

B

C

8 DAYS
PUSH AIR
WARNING
THE FOLLOWING MANIFOLD PRESSURES ARE MAX IMUM FOR OPERATION AND SHOULD NOT BE EXCEEDED
MARKER BEACON
CLIMB
PUSH
SELECTOR VALVE
ALTERNATE SOURCE
PILOTS OXYGEN
BLINKER
OXYGEN FLOW INDICATOR
AIL LOCK
MANIFOLD PRESSURE SELECTOR
LOCK
CLOSED

390th Collection

390th Collection

A

B

David A. Tyler

Previous page: *The main instrument panel of the B-17. Center cluster contains the instruments for flying through the murk that often blanketed England. At right are the engine performance gauges. Directly in front of the pilot is the Pilot Directional Indicator (PDI), whose needle was to be kept centered during the bomb run.*

A. *Throttle technique in the B-17 required a palm-up grasp of the quadrant. According to the AAF manual, throttles handled in this fashion could be smoothly and evenly advanced to takeoff power.*

B. *The pilot was commander of the bomber and the crew.*

C. *During long flights the copilot would relieve the pilot from tiresome formation flying. He also kept track of the engines, fuel usage, crew reports, and injuries.*

D. *The center pedestal held throttle and propeller controls on the top. Below are the auto pilot control switches. When engaged, the bomber was effectively flown by the bombardier through the bombsight operated in conjunction with the auto pilot. Red handle at bottom right locked the tail wheel before takeoff. Red handle at bottom left was the rudder and elevator control lock.*

D

A

A. *The senior enlisted crew member was the flight engineer and top turret gunner. During takeoff, he assisted the pilots in monitoring the engines and systems. As the bomber approached hostile airspace, he climbed into the top turret.*

B. *From this position atop the bomber the gunner's responsibility was to cover the sky above and call out the position of attacking fighters for the other gunners.*

C. *Interior of the top turret. Switches control power to the electrically operated turret and ammunition feed system for the twin .50-caliber machine guns.*

D. *Large, yellow, low-pressure bottles held oxygen supplies for the crew. The silver box contained the inter phone jack through which the crew communicated. Mounted on the bulkhead to the right is the electrical fuse panel the engineer monitored during the mission.*

Overleaf: *The top turret gunner's view to the 6 o'clock position. This early turret was an enclosure of steel and Plexiglas that provided a surprisingly restricted view. Later turrets were completely enclosed in Plexiglas, affording far better visibility.*

B

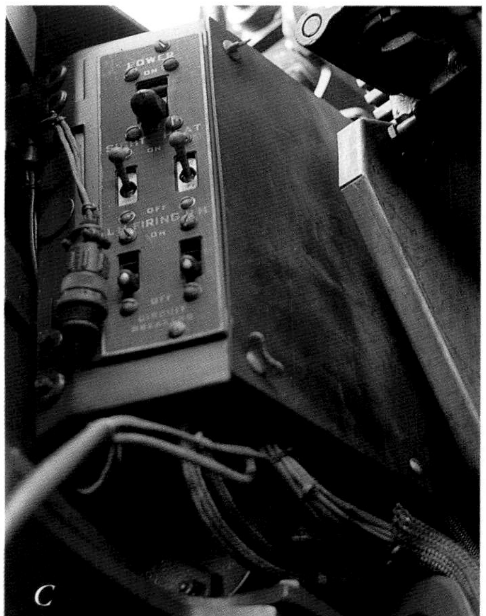

C

390th Collection

D

A

A. Looking aft through the bomb bay. Bomb racks created a very strong structure in the center of the bomber. The narrow catwalk was the only route fore and aft. This pathway had to be traversed while wearing full high-altitude clothing and lugging a portable oxygen bottle. The journey might be made with the bomber under attack by fighters and flak — the bomb bay doors swung open to the earth 20,000+ feet below. At top right are the control cables that connect the flight deck to the control surfaces in the tail. Through the bulkhead doors one can view the support structure for the ball turret — its yellow oxygen bottle attached.

B. Looking from inside the bomb bay towards the cockpit. Numbered bomb shackles correspond to lights on the bombardier's control panel. At lower left is a bright green walk-around oxygen bottle. These portable bottles could be refilled by the main oxygen system at an outlet at every crew station.

C. Electrically actuated bomb bay doors were opened as the bomber approached the target. Pilots often asked the bombardier to delay opening until the last possible moment because their considerable drag slowed the bomber. Electrical cut-out switches made bomb release impossible unless the doors were fully open.

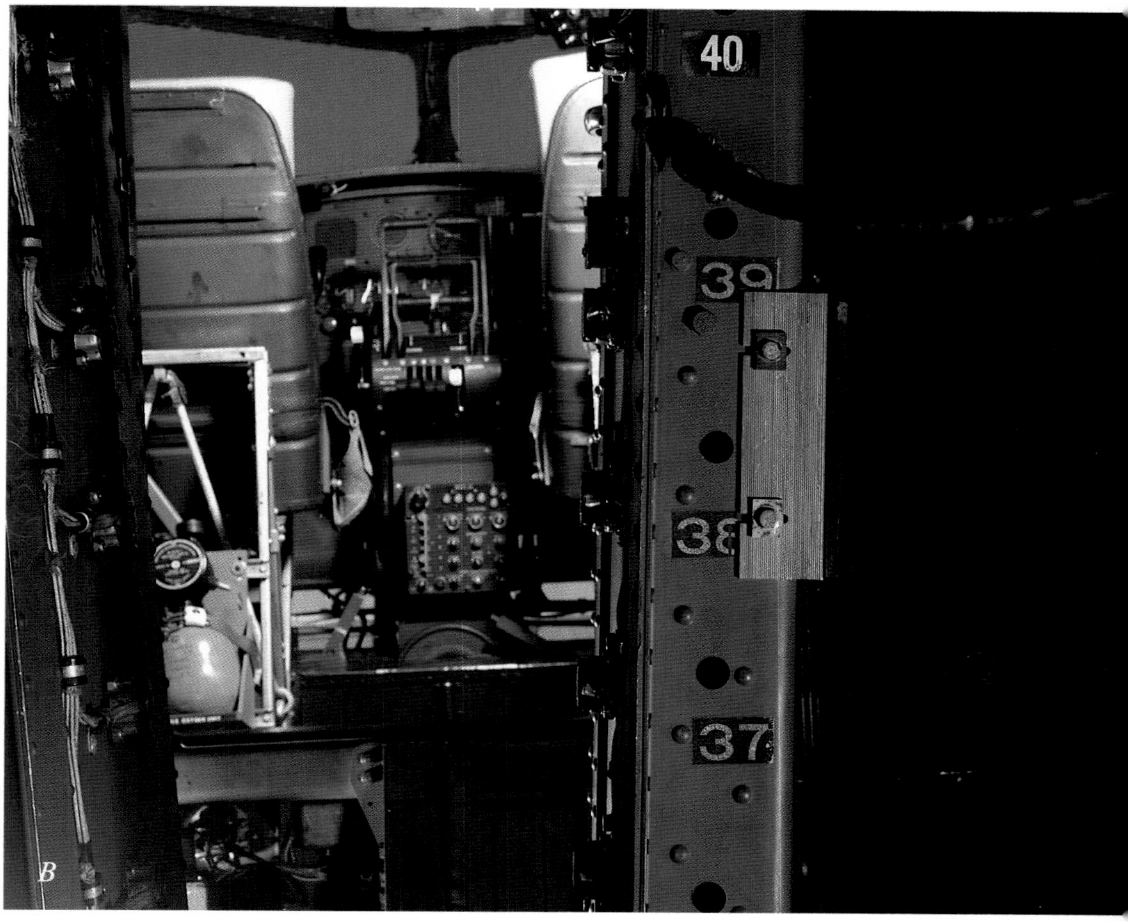

David A. Tyler

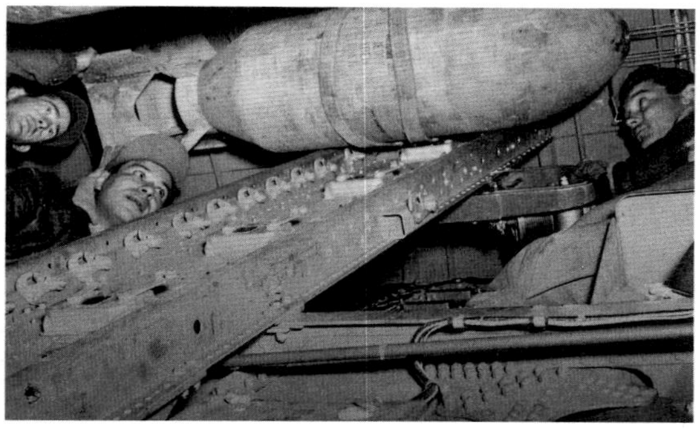

USAFM

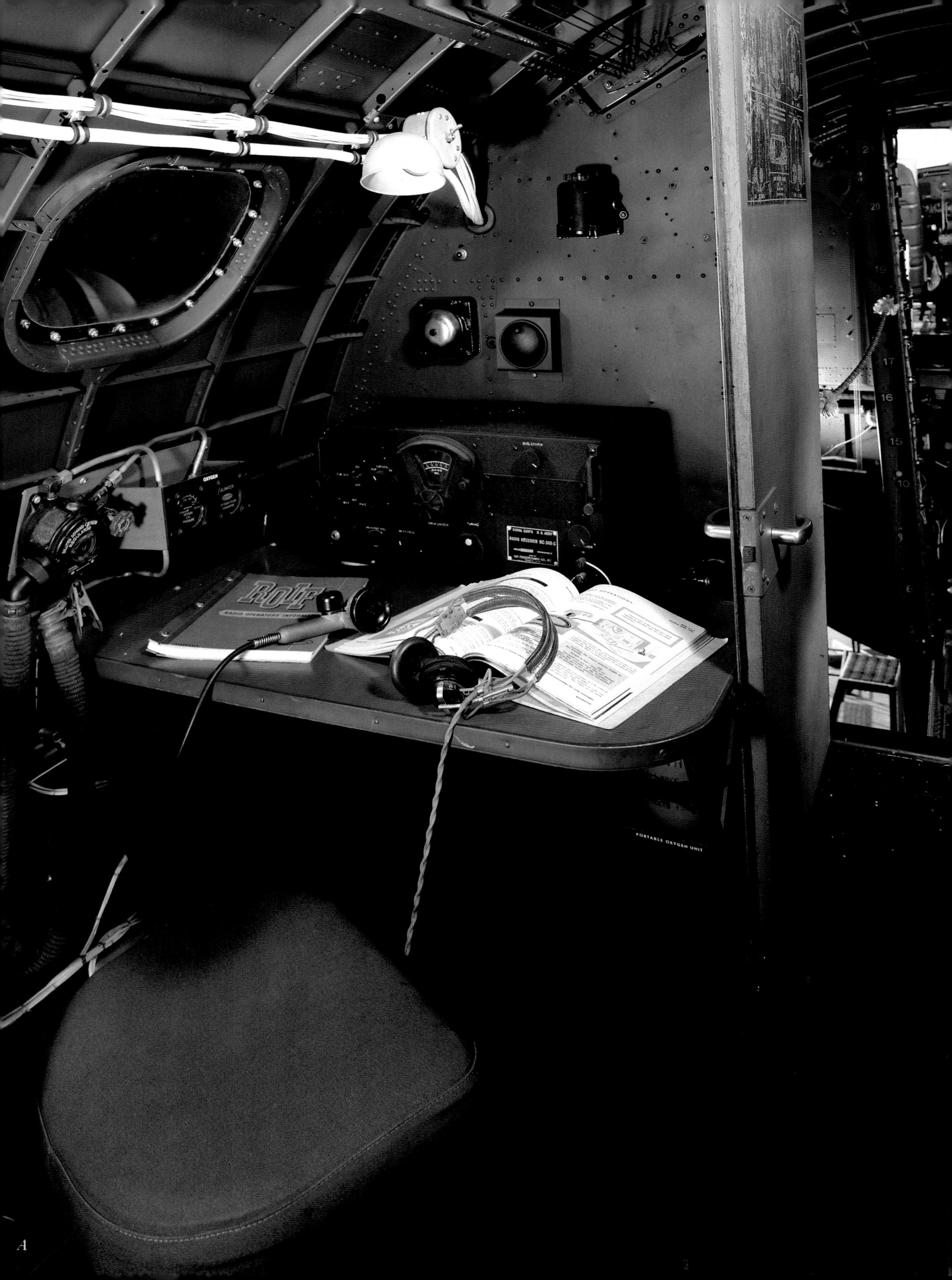

A

A. The radio operator's position in the center of the bomber just aft the bomb bay. Besides his communication duties, the radio operator ran cameras mounted below the floor of his station. Camera aircraft were randomly positioned throughout the formations to record the strike. Operated via an intervalometer, the cameras fired every few seconds as the bombs fell and impacted.

Both photos USAFM

B. Looking aft from the radio operator's outside hatch. Early B-17s had a single .50-caliber machine gun here on a flexible mount. These guns proved ineffective and were later eliminated.

C. The radio operator's telegraph key. In addition to large and heavy radio receivers and transmitters, he used Morse code and this most basic tool.

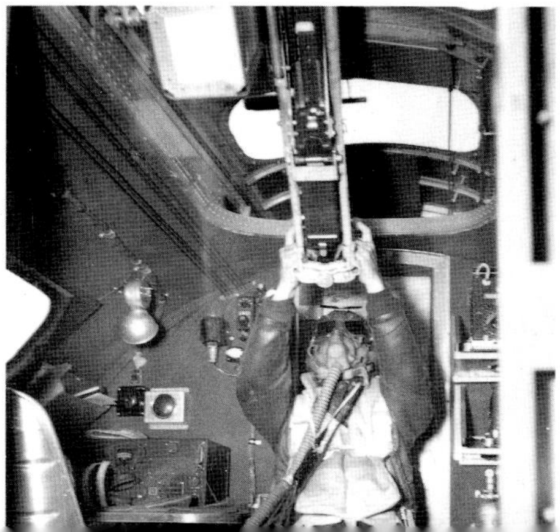

A

A. Looking towards 6 o'clock position from inside the ball turret. Enclosed in a sphere of glass and steel, suspended below the fuselage, the ball turret gunner guarded the bomber's belly. At left is the barrel of one of his two .50-caliber machine guns.

B. The Sperry ball turret.

C. This was the ball turret gunner's view as he entered his position. The ball turret, to be entered, had to be positioned with the guns pointed straight down. This exposed a hatch to the inside of the B-17. The gunner stepped into the heel plates and curled himself into the ball. The turret sight was straight ahead. Once inside and the hatch closed behind — the ball turret gunner was alone in his sphere, communicating with his crewmates only through the inter phone. Below are the charging handles for arming the machine guns.

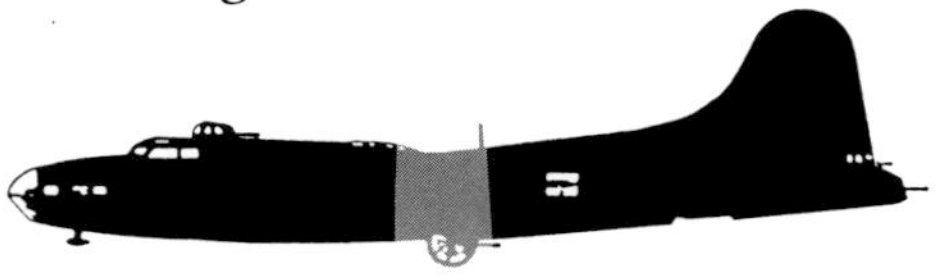

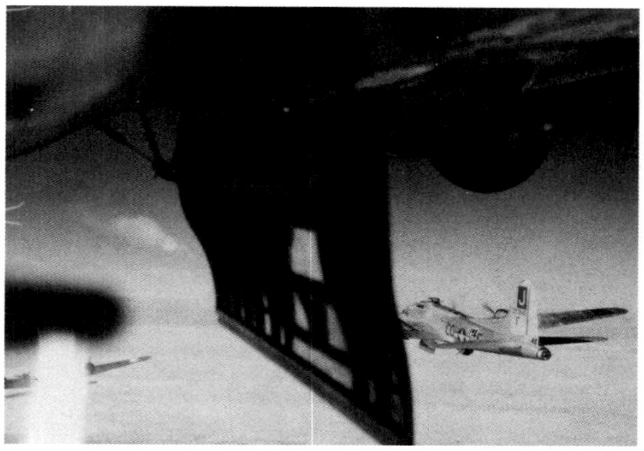

390th Collection

David A. Tyler

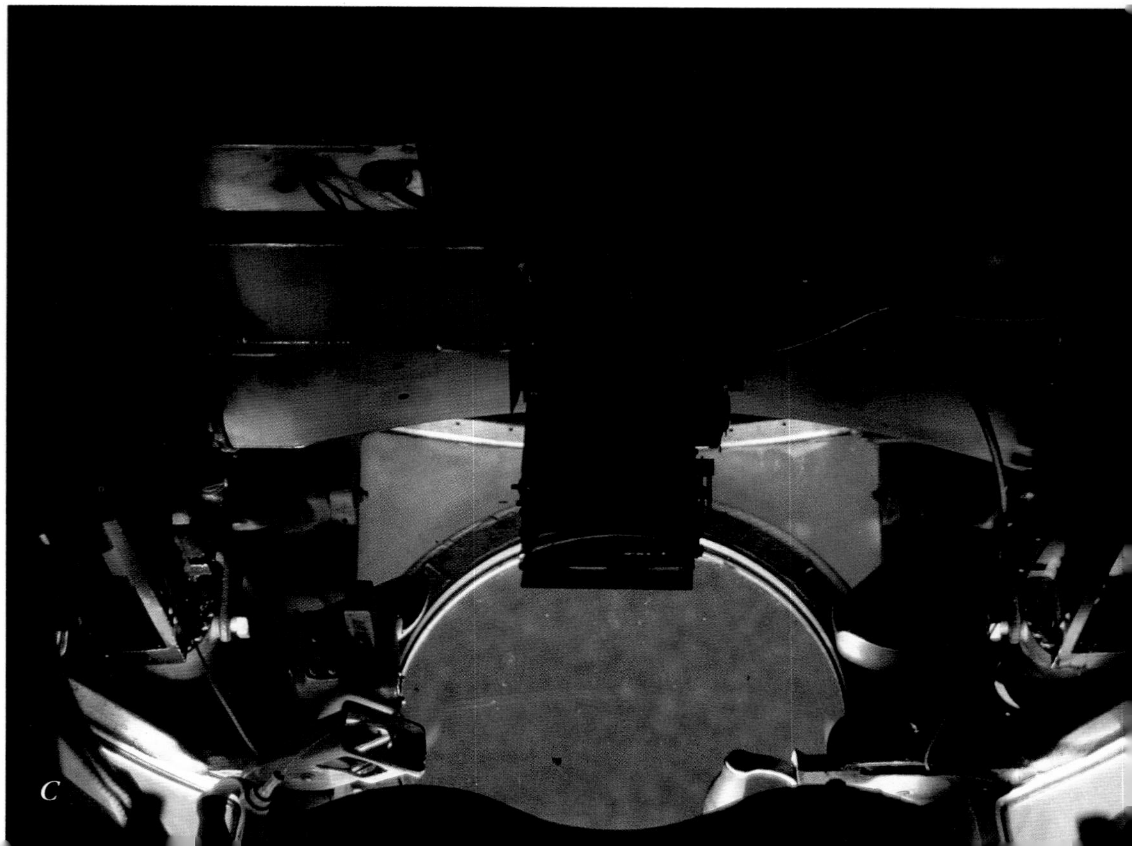

A

Previous page: Waist gunners had to fight the slipstream to maneuver these 65-pound guns throughout their range of travel while leading incoming fighters and remembering not to shoot parts off their own aircraft. Earlier versions of the B-17 had these men directly opposite each other. Later B-17G models staggered their positions.

A. Right waist gunner's view to the 4 o'clock position. Early WWII B-17s had open waist windows that let a 150+ MPH slipstream howl through the rear of the bomber. Later B-17Gs had enclosed windows with guns mounted in a flexible ball-type fitting. In a stowed position is the gunner's single .50-caliber machine gun.

B. Looking forward from the main entry door through the waist area up to the ball turret support structure. The large plywood box at right contained ammunition for the right waist gun. The flexible track kept the belts of .50-caliber ammunition feeding smoothly to the gun. After a mission the floor would be filled with brass casings.

C. Looking inside through the left waist position. Forward the waist window is a retractable wind deflector. Gunners would often stencil their kills below the station.

B

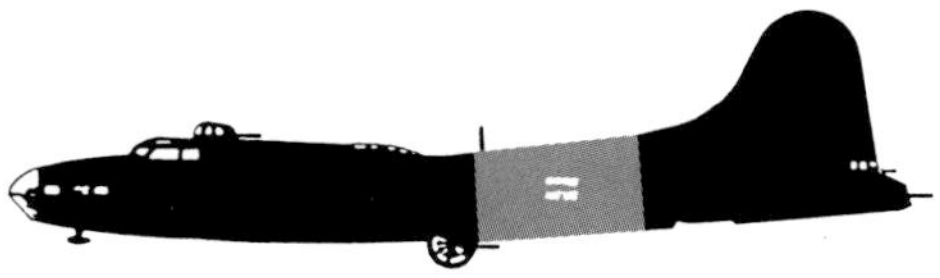

C

A

A. The tail gunner was responsible for protecting the rear area. His station, directly below the large rudder, afforded him a panoramic view of the air battle as it unfolded. Lead bombers would sometimes station an officer or pilot in this position to keep the air group commander apprised of the formation condition. Seen here is the early ring and bead gunsight that rose and fell with the movement of the guns. The entire aiming assembly was connected to the guns by cables. Later B-17s had reflector gunsights and rounded station enclosures.

B. Interior of the tail gun position. The tail gunner spent hours sitting or kneeling upon a bicycle-type seat, reaching around the armor plate to handle the guns.

C. The tail gunner's oxygen control panel. Crewmen had to monitor a blinker gauge that indicated oxygen flow. Ice would sometimes form in the masks or hoses and slowly cut off the oxygen supply. A man did not last long at 25,000 feet without oxygen.

Overleaf: The tail gunner in the last bomber of the formation, the low squadron of the low group, had this view as the bomber stream moved into enemy airspace. Sometimes called the "Purple Heart Corner," the bomber in this position would often be the first attacked by enemy fighters.

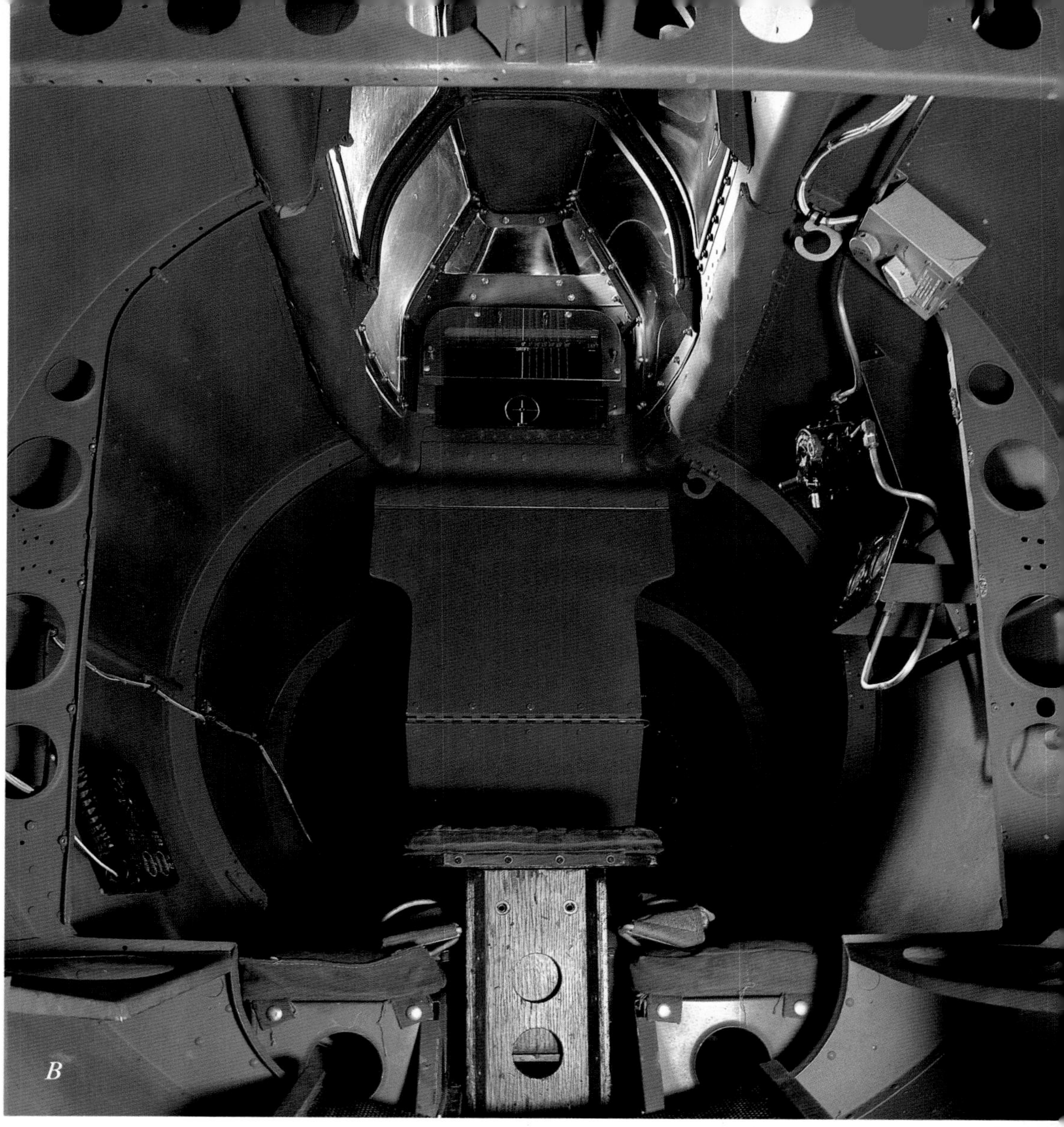

B

C

A

A. The ground crews had many preflight activities to prepare the bombers for a mission. The engines needed to have their propellers pulled through before start-up. This procedure cleared the lower cylinders of oil that had pooled since the last flight.

B. The engines and associated systems received attention from the line crews up to the time of engine start.

C. Often the crew chief felt the air crews were only borrowing "his" bomber to fly a mission. These men, often older than the air crews, added their experience and improvisational skills to keep these machines in the air.

B

Both photos David A. Tyler

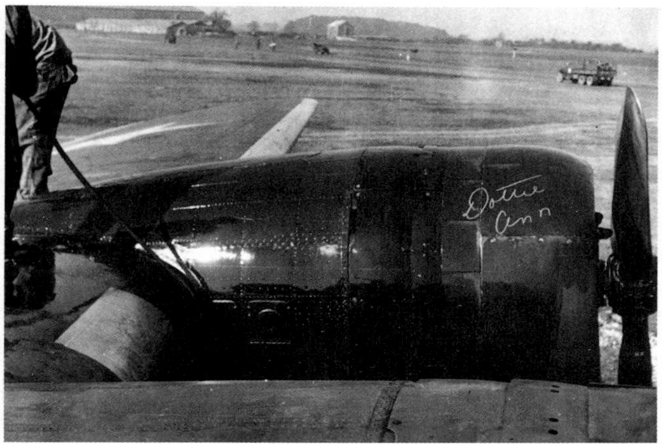

C

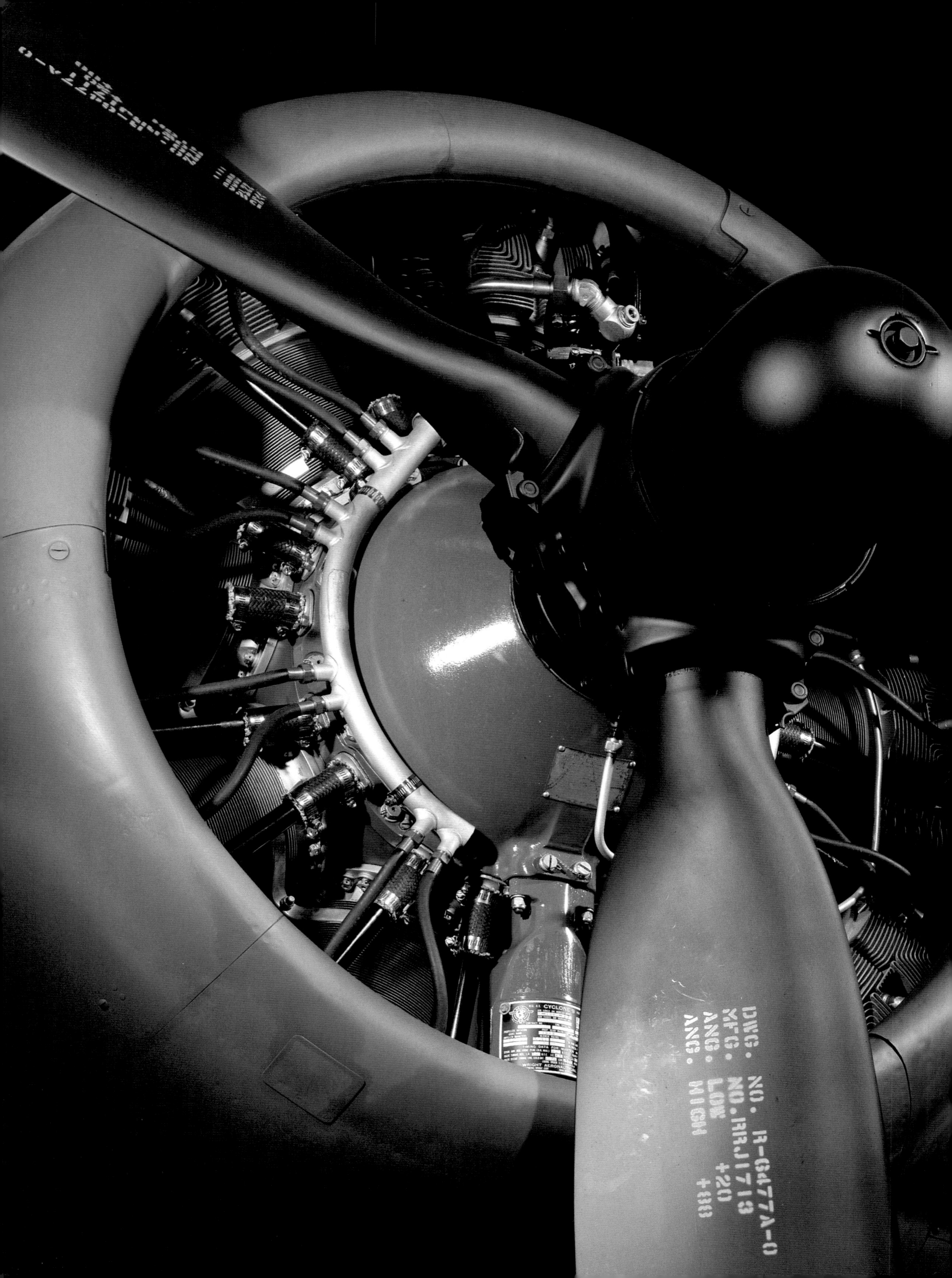
DWG. NO. R-6477A-0
MFG. NO. RRJ1713
ANG. LOW +20
ANG. HIGH +88

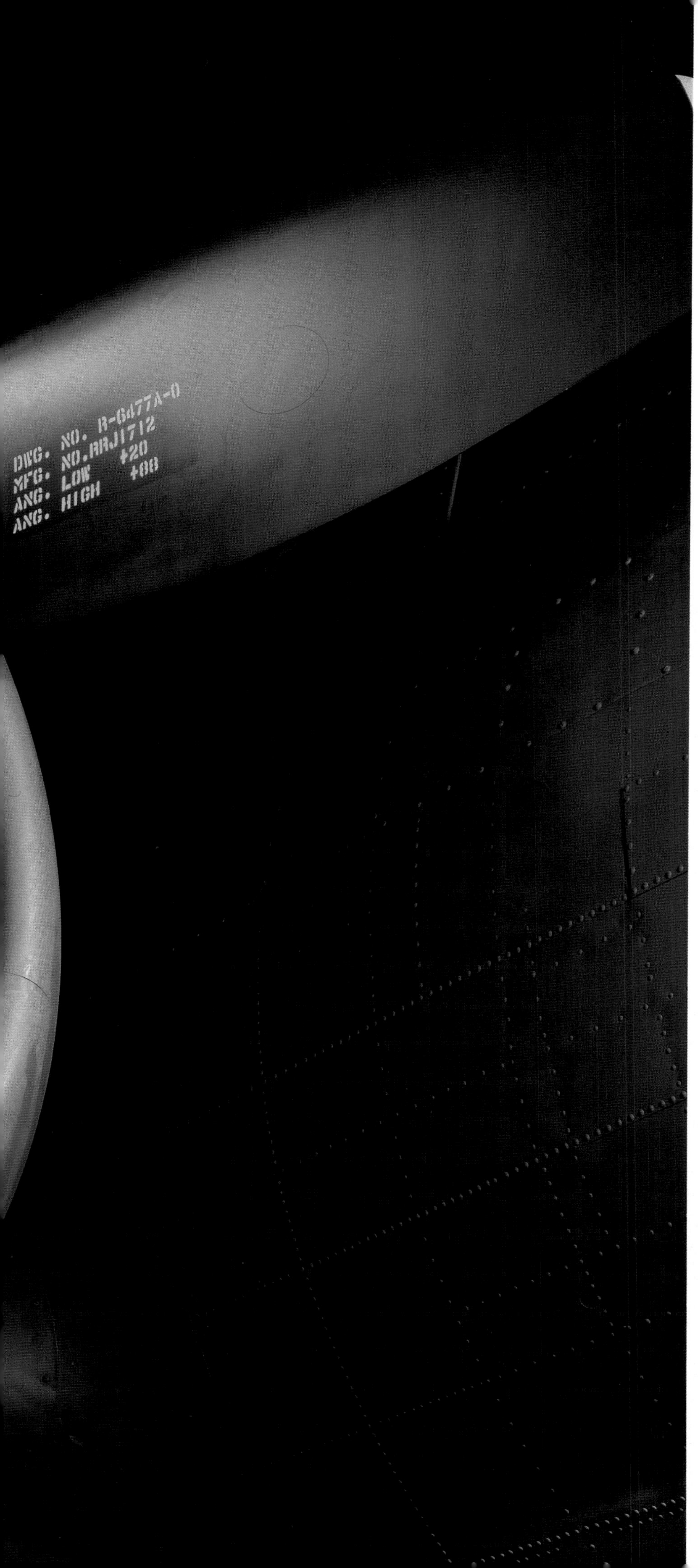

The Wright Cyclone R-1820 developed 1,200 horsepower spinning a 500-pound Hamilton Standard propeller. Oil stains on the cowling were a common sight. Each of these radial engines had a 38-gallon oil tank. A former crew chief, when asked about the oil stains, stated, " If there ain't any oil on it — there ain't any oil in it!"

Both photos 390th Collection

8 91 BG
401 BS 7

Line crews and armorers serviced the turrets and guns between missions, in all kinds of weather.

USAFM

David A. Tyler

A

A. Rain was a constant problem for the men of Eighth Air Force. Missions were often flown in less than ideal conditions. Ground crews worked through the rain, dark, cold, and mud to keep "their" bombers mission-ready.

B. The pilot's walk-around inspection included a review of Form 1A. This listed the work that needed to be done on the bomber and the attention it had received from the ground crew.

C. One of the ten fuel caps through which the B-17's 2,700-gallon fuel capacity flowed. Self - sealing tanks made of multiple rubber layers saved countless bomber crews.

B

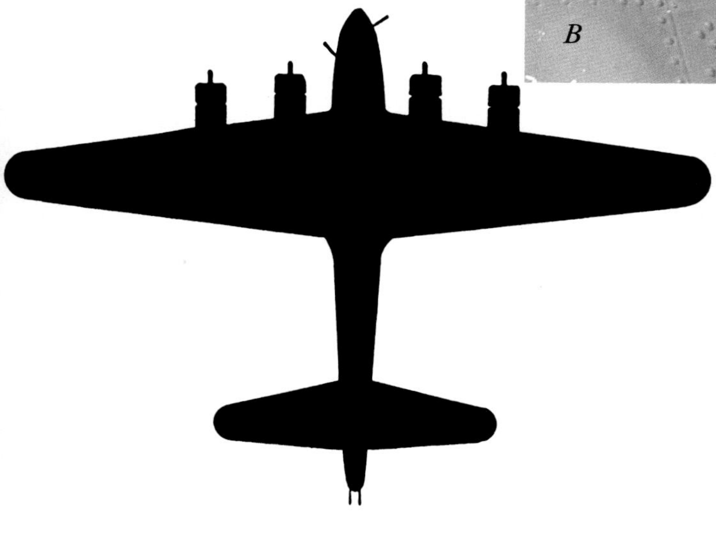

David A. Tyler

C

K

Crews often had to sweat out a mission start next to their bombers on hardstands dispersed across the airbases. Missions were sometimes delayed due to weather over England or the target. Delays could upset the intricate process of formation assembly and escort rendezvous.

David A. Tyler

A

A. At one point during the daylight bomber offensive, replacement crews were being lost so soon after arriving that base commanders ordered crew photos of all the new crews before their first mission, so that they could place faces with the names of the missing.

B. and C. Crewmen checked and rechecked the tools of their trade until climbing aboard to begin the mission.

B

Both photos USAFM

C

A F
777

Memphis Belle

Acknowledgments

This book would be not have been possible without the participation of David Tallichet. He provided the opportunity to travel back through time in his B-17. The majority of the photographs were done in the plane that he owns and operates, most famous for its portrayal of the *Memphis Belle* in the recent film. He has restored this plane to the configuration of the early bomber raids of 1943. I am indebted to him for the opportunity to make these photos in what is almost an operational B-17, and on a personal basis for allowing me to live my childhood dream...not only to ride in a B-17 but to sit in the left seat and fly.

Rosann, my wife, and the kids Nate, Brigitta, and Joe for persevering with me as this project took some ups and downs. Paul Perkins, a lifelong friend.

Ross Howell and Howell Press, what else can I say but thanks for believing in the value of this concept.

Joe Ventolo Jr. and Michelle Crean for the historical research. The opening paragraph is a recount of a story told to Joe Ventolo Jr. by Joe Ventolo Sr. who was employed at Wright Field and saw "The Lady" depart the runway for parts unknown.

Ron Dick, Air Vice Marshall RAF(retired), who took the time to look this over, make suggestions, and provide some early support.

Jeff Ethell, whose efforts to point me in the right direction finally led me here.

United States Air Force Museum director Colonel Richard Uppstrom, USAF(retired), for the initial access to *Shoo Shoo Baby* and an unending reference library. Also to the men in Dover, Delaware, who restored *Shoo Shoo Baby*, Ray McCloskey, Tom Corbeil, Dan Vassey, and Vic Rosica. Also in Delaware, Maryellis Jenkins.

"Dutch" Biel, photographer with the 390th Bomb Group and commercial photographer in Dayton, Ohio. His time and access to his files and memory continue to be invaluable.

David A. Tyler, pilot with the 305th Bomb Group, for access to his unique scrapbook. Darryl Griffing for helping to make the connection.

The National Warplane Museum in Geneseo, New York, which operates B-17G, *Fuddy Duddy*, the Arizona wing of the Confederate Air Force, which operates B-17G, *Sentimental Journey*, the Texas Wing of the CAF, which operates B-17G, *Texas Raiders*. The late O.K. Coulter.

I would like to also thank Jim Sullivan, Shelly Mulvaine, Mia Kosicki, John and Bonnie Knab, Steve Lipofsky, Mike Ripley, John Hess, Steve Jennings, "Pony" Maples, Simon Forty, David Hake, Chris Peatridge, Dick Baughman, Dave Menard, and Wes Henry.

Technical Notes

The original photography in this book was all done with the intent to as faithfully as possible remove the clues of the present day and try to look back through a window opened by the owners and operators of these aircraft, a window into the 1940s when formations of these airplanes flew over the European continent during World War II.

I used a variety of cameras and equipment to complete this project: a Wista 4x5 Field View camera, with a 150mm Caltar II lens and a 90mm Nikkor lens; a Mamiya RB67 with 50mm, 90mm, and 180mm lenses; and a Nikon F3 with a motor drive and a garden variety of Nikkor lenses.

All the photographs were shot as transparencies to make the best possible color separations.

The 4x5 and 6x7 photos were all shot on Kodak Ektachrome Daylight film. The 35mm photos were all taken with Kodachrome 200.

This book was designed and produced on a PC clone using Aldus Pagemaker 4.0; the typeface is Garamond. The concept, design, and the photographs are done by Dan Patterson, 6825 Peters Pike, Dayton, Ohio 45414.

The Association of Living History, comprising the crewmen in these photographs, is an organization that is dedicated to the preservation and remembrance of the aircrews of the Second World War. The association provides historically accurate crewmen and women for airshows featuring the aircraft of World War II. Each member carefully researches the background, uniform, and crew positions to create a realistic impression of the soldiers who flew and fought in the airplanes of the 1940s.

Their input and technical advice were invaluable as this project evolved.

Bombardier	Dave Berry
Navigator	Troy Mulvaine
Pilot	Tom Kosicki
Copilot	Bruce Zeigler
Top Turret	Jim O'Neil
Radio	Tom Horton
Ball Turret	Jim Kindred
Left Waist	Kurt Weidner
Right Waist	Andre Bone
Tail	Chris Lehman
Crewmen	Jonathan Lewis
	Mike Noonan
	Hugh Daly
	Dale Burrier

Bibliography

BOOKS:

AAF. *Official World War II Guide to the Army Air Forces.* New York: Bonanza Books, 1988.

Andrade, John M. *U.S. Military Aircraft Designations and Serials Since 1909.* England: Midland Counties Publications (Aerophile), 1979.

Bowers, Peter M. *Boeing Aircraft Since 1916.* London: Putnam & Company, 1966.

__________. *50th Anniversary Boeing B-17 Flying Fortress.* Museum of Flight, 1985.

Bowman, Martin. *Castles in the Air: the Story of the B-17 Flying Fortress Crews of the US 8th Air Force.* England: Patrick Stephens, 1984.

Byers, Richard G. *Attack.* Fayetteville, Arkansas: Aardvark Press, 1984.

Byers, Roland O. *Flak Dodger.* Moscow, Idaho: Pawpaw Press, 1985.

__________. *Black Puff Polly.* Moscow, Idaho: Pawpaw Press, 1991.

Caidin, Martin. *Black Thursday.* New York: Bantam Books, 1981.

__________. *Flying Forts: the B-17 in World War II.* New York: Bantam Books, 1990.

Comer, John. *Combat Crew.* New York: Pocket Books, 1989.

Dorr, Robert F. *U. S. Bombers of World War II.* London:Arms & Armour Press, 1989.

Ethell, Jeffrey L. and Alfred Price. *Target Berlin.* London: Arms & Armour Press, 1989.

Ethell, Jeffrey L.; Grinsell, Robert; Freeman, Roger; Anderton, David A.; Johnsen, Frederick A; Vangas-Baginskis, Alex; and Mikesh, Robert C. *The Great Book of World War II Airplanes.* New York: Bonanza Books, 1984.

Freeman, Roger A. *B-17 Fortress At War.* New York: Charles Scribner's Sons, 1977.

Heflin, Woodford Agee, ed. *United States Air Force Dictionary.* Air University Press, 1956.

Higham, Robin, and Carol Williams, ed. *Flying Combat Aircraft of the USAAF- USA Vol. 2.* Ames, Iowa: Iowa State University Press, 1978.

Jablonski, Edward. *Flying Fortress.* New York: Doubleday, 1965.

LeMay, General Curtis E., with MacKinlay Kantor. *Mission With LeMay.* Garden City, New York: Doubleday & Company, 1965.

Lloyd, Alwyn T. *B-17 Flying Fortress Part 2: Derivatives.* Fallbrook, California: Aero Publishers, 1983.

Lloyd, Alwyn T. *B-17 Flying Fortress Part 3: More Derivatives.* Fallbrook, California: Aero Publishers, 1983.

O'Neill, Brian D. *Half a Wing, Three Engines, and a Prayer: B-17s Over Germany.* Blue Ridge Summit, Pennsylvania: AERO, Division of TAB Books 1989.

Polmar, Norman, ed. *Strategic Air Command: People, Aircraft, and Missiles.* Annapolis, Maryland: The Nautical and Aviation Publishing Company of America, 1979.

Smith, Maj. Gen. Dale O. *Screaming Eagles: Memoirs of a B-17 Group Commander.* Chapel Hill, N. C.: Algonquin Books, 1990.

Spick, Mike. *Fighter Pilot Tactics.* Cambridge, England: Patrick Stephens, 1983.

Sunderman, Col. James F., ed. *World War II in the Air: Pacific.* New York: Van Nostrand Reinhold Company, 1981.

Swanborough, Gordon and Peter M. Bowers. *United States Military Aircraft Since 1909.* Washington, D. C.: Smithsonian Institution Press, 1989.

Watry, Charles A. and Duane L. Hall. *Aerial Gunners: the Unknown Aces of World War II.* Carlsbad, California: California Aero Press, 1986.

PERIODICALS:

Ardman, Harvey. "The Flying Fortress of World War II." *The American Legion Magazine,* November 1972.

Blue, Allan G. "Round Peg in a Square Hole." *Flying Review International,* October 1965.

Chapman, John, and Geoff Goodall. *Warbirds Worldwide Directory.* Warbirds Worldwide, n.d.

DeGroat, Robert S. "Geneseo '88." *Warbirds,* November/December 1989.

Fosdick, Dean. "Turboprops Replace Aging Firebombers." *The Herald-Palladium,* St. Joseph, Michigan, 14 August 1991.

George, Lt. Gen. Harold L. "Aerospace Profile: The Most Outstanding Leader." *Aerospace Historian,* Summer 1968.

Paul Perkins (left) and Dan Patterson (right). Rosann Patterson

Dan Patterson is a self-employed photographer and graphic designer living in Dayton, Ohio. His first book, *Shoo Shoo Baby, A Lucky Lady of the Sky,* is also about a B-17.

Paul Perkins is an emergency room physician living in Yellow Springs, Ohio.